KALTENHOUSE
REMEMBERED

NORMAN A. THOMPSON

outskirts
press

Outskirts Press, Inc.
http://www.outskirtspress.com

ISBN: 978-1-9772-2473-6

U.S. Copyright Registration Number: TX 8-776-347

TABLE OF CONTENTS

FOREWORD

While sitting around in various *Rainbow Division Veterans Association* reunion rap sessions, I have noted that it has been only in the latter years of the lives of many combat veterans that they have had either the will or want to recall their military past, and indeed, to talk about it.

Perhaps it has been something which they wished not to remember, or perhaps it was something they would rather forget, which brought about this phenomenon.

However, I feel that we had other things that prioritized our time. We had professions to pursue, women to love and families to raise.

Perhaps it was a little of each along with other psychological underlyingcauses that prompted us to maintain our silence.

However, most of us have mellowed and lost the

trauma of war, and in the vernacular of those kids and grandkids we have raised, we are ready to "let it all hang out."

We can now talk of failures equally with jobs well done. In that vein, I have been compelled to write these pages about those Rainbow troops and their experiences in an attempt to record a part of history that they so valiantly played.

This, the story of Kaltenhouse, is about one brief segment of our effort to survive and accomplish the ultimate victory.

THE AUTHOR

TROOPS OF G242

THE WRONG BODY language, fragile frayed nerves, an expression of nervousness, or just the lack of an outward show of "daring do" may overshadow the bravery of a soldier's actions and a true hero may easily go unheralded.

So it was, in their "moments of truth" and "times for decision" that men and boys such as Leonard Shepherd, Darrell Martin, Robert Spearing III, Charles Paine and Lloyd Teale shared such human frailties.

Those who knew them recognized what they had done was done willingly without the need for praise and/or glorification.

One uniquely individual trait seemed to prevail in the character of each of them. Each knew and understood that he had a certain task to do and that task was something from which there would be no running: they could not, they wouldn't, even though chances were that they probably wanted to.

For that reason and others, they, through the mysterious ways of the military, had been chosen to lead with individual commands as small as a five-man mortar squad to as large as a rifle company. It didn't really matter as each responded in his own private, positive way.

So it was that narrowing dark eyes, stammered words, and quick glances over tensed shoulders would come to belie Sergeant Darrell "Dee Dee" Martin's posture as a leader of men.

He was to me, however, as were the others, a tad braver than the many brave men I warmly recall as "Rainbow." He was Platoon Sergeant, Weapons Platoon, G Company, Second Battalion, 242nd Infantry Regiment of the 42nd "Rainbow" Division, my outfit.

Sarge's bravery most certainly wouldn't be measured by an outward show of dauntless, intrepid valor. That was the kids bent on playing Cowboys and Indians. They never understood the rationale of war and that its offering of death was real. He was, after all, an "Old Fart" born in 1917 and at least eight years older than most of us. Hell, he was all of twenty-seven at the time.

Dee Dee's inner courage and strength were evidenced in his knowing when and how to muster up the qualities most needed when circumstances had put him on the line. This was never more evident than during the events that took place during our winter defense of the small village of Kaltenhouse, France between January 21 and January 27, 1945.

Staff Sergeant Bob Spearing was a squad leader in Tech Sergeant Art Stuemke's third platoon, was married with two very young sons and his family history was eerily sprinkled with the military.

His father, Robert Spearing Jr., was a much-decorated WWI Navy veteran. His uncle, Lt. Commander Joe Madison, had lost a leg as skipper of the troop transport Ticonderoga and in 1918 received the Congressional Medal of Honor. Bob did not particularly seek glory and, in fact, professed to seek nothing more of the military than past membership in the Boy Scouts.

Dark tight wavy hair combined with even darker piercing eyes complemented the confidence of my squad leader, Lloyd Teale. An ASTP transfer to "Rainbow," Lloyd oozed college. The guys he hung with oozed college, and together they intimidated the rest of us in the section, which was only three, my buddy "Willie," Dee Dee and me.

"Willie," Warren "Gene" Willson, was a southern Oregon ranch kid a couple of years older than I. He was married with a daughter he had hardly come to know, a trucker and farmer in civilian life and proud of it.

Charlie "Lank" Paine shipped over as a platoon guide. Now within 24 hours he had become platoon sergeant, and then acting platoon leader. Soon he would receive his bars with a battlefield commission.

Charlie spoke of his "non-duties" as a staff sergeant stateside platoon guide. On-field problems he recalled "popping" around seemingly busy but mostly doing nothing. He just sort of tagged along as a "spare tire" to perform whatever tasks came his way, while Lt. Shepard, Sgt. Sam McGill and their subordinate squad leaders did all the normal chain of command platoon work.

He notes now that the army in all its wisdom and knowledge of statistics made note of the inordinate losses of tech sergeants and second lieutenants in combat rifle platoons. As a result, the position of platoon guide was born; a staff sergeant who could usually be found in a safe place, available to be shot at when "his" time came around. In the meantime, he could follow behind everyone else, watch for stragglers and "prod and kick ass."

Actually things never worked quite the way they were supposed to with Lank. The first day out as rearguard, fulfilling his required duties as the last man in the "whole damn company," a single shot ricocheted just in front of him. So much for the safety of the rear echelon.

However, as a rifle platoon noncom, he was no stranger to us in Weapons. Tall, slim and bespectacled, he always seemed to be where the action was, and despite his unassuming manner, he always appeared to be in control. When inducted I, Norm Thompson, was freshly married to a freshly pregnant little redhead of seventeen named Margie Voeks. At only eighteen years of age I was handed a military high school diploma, given fourteen weeks basic, another fourteen as a cadre, and along with my buddy "Willie" was pushed into a five-man mortar squad, three squad section with a dozen ASTP. Neither Willie nor I had ever fired a mortar round.

Norm and Margie wedding

Norm and Willie

Willie and I were the last to fill out the squad and were assigned as ammo bearers. Ammo bearers were considered the lesser of the least and hardly earned the rank of buck private, we were surely meant to perpetuate the term "dogface."

Lieutenants Robert Daly and Robert "Bob" Collins; First Sergeant Paul Graham; riflemen Jerry Ford; Clint Murphy, Glenn DeVoge, Glenn Domino, Claude Hawkins, Harvey Kent, Bob King, Tom Crosson and Johnny Frasell; BAR Ed Gall; weapons guys Bill Kenny, Bill Nickeson, and George Atkins; and our own weapons "Kraut Command," including Ray Schumacher, Richard Schmidtman, and Clarence Schneider, each webbed his way in and out of their own unique part of this military history.

Tom O'Neill, Glenn Martin, my section sergeant, Phil Schaeffer, and Wayne Scott, who gave his life at Kaltenhouse—each recorded individually in the following chapters.

During all major conflicts, even those of worldwide proportions, the enormity of it all would often end up confined to brief moments in time and of very little space. Historical tides changed in fleeting moments.

At any one specific minute of any specific day of one specific week of every period in military history there was always a coinciding specific theater of operations, specific army group, a specific division and on through: regiment, battalion, company, platoon, squad and finally that one specific foot soldier who would make the difference.

Perhaps that would be a scout out front for his platoon searching for contact. Or a search and destroy patrol five hundred yards from the main line of resistance (MLR)… or a Company of troops such as ours holding a perimeter of defense against an enemy stronghold such as Oberhoffen.

KOENIGSBRUCK

Early the morning of January 15, shortly after the gut-wrenching Gambsheim and Hatten-Rittershoffen conflict, G Company was pulled from its quiet defense of Niederbetsdorf and assembled at a staging area for movement to Koenigsbruck, some twenty kilometers east.

It was a quiet ride in the six-bys which transported us over winding dirt roads and across the rolling wooded Vosges foothills to just outside the village.

We were fatigued and battle-weary, and, ill-equipped both mentally and physically for another immediate battle.

Our uneasiness of anticipating another Gambsheim or Hatten was dispelled by the quiet serenity offered by the Haguenau timberland with its deep green pines and bright foliage. A fresh rain and a continuing drizzle left a pristine freshness about. A warm chinook like wind had melted away most of the light snow.

Koenigsbruck was smaller than most Haguenau Forest villages and our company lines were to border the entire northern edge of town facing the Germans.

Their battalion MLR was now extended precariously 20 kilometers out from the other allied lines.

With a pair of H Company heavy 30's in support, G Company entered the village and set about securing our new positions.

Our riflemen took prior diggings of those combatants from Love Company who had seen action in the village before. There were slit trenches, two-man holes and earthen bunkers all along the line.

The two H Company heavy 30's took gun placements at the two extreme flanks. Our rifle troops and light 30's were out, singularly spaced and several yards apart.

Telephone lines were strung from our MLR to single man outposts two hundred yards out and across the open meadow to a tree line directly to the front. A four-hour stint at one of these outposts was a most telling experience for any poor "sonuvabitch" unlucky enough to pull such duty.

From their diggings on the line, the riflemen could peer out over the defilade offered by their slight elevation and across the open fields to the wooded area beyond.

The meadow was guarded by knee-high, heavy grasses and offered cover for an enemy either real or imagined.

This was in the truest essence, a "no man's land," created from their side by way of heavy armor and outposts, and from ours by way of our well-secured MLR, the flanking H Company heavy 30's and a great number of reconnaissance patrols. We held our Koenigsbruck positions in relative quiet with that exception.

However, duty, especially at night, at those lonely outposts near or just inside the wood line took their toll on already strained nerves.

The imaginary enemy always outnumbered the real; every night sound was magnified and succinctly spelled out imminent danger. Statuesque stumps could be seen moving about, inching their way forward. Clumps of brush were Jerry patrols lying in wait for the slightest movement. Even breathing seemed a threat.

Lt. Collins and Shepherd were the two remaining line officers in the company. The loss of the leadership of Lt. "Big John" Salopek during that second day out at Gambsheim was of tremendous import to all of us. He was one officer to whom every man in his platoon and most of the company felt an inherent allegiance.

Our Company CO, Capt. Bernard Reiter, had been given a regimental staff position, and Lt. Daly had been assigned to F Company at Hatten.

Machine Gun Section Sergeant, "Dee Dee" Martin was now the ranking noncom in Weapons with Sgt. "Bromo" Sultzer carried on the roster as MIA.

With Lt. Daly gone, Dee Dee had assumed the roles of both Platoon Sergeant and Platoon Leader.

Sgt. Phil Schaeffer billeted our Mortar Section in a cottage adjacent to a canal that bisected the village with our OP in a tall rickety grist mill nearby. The gun placements were set up with the grist mill as defilade.

The mill itself was the tallest building in the village with its shaft negotiable by circular wooden stairs running to a platform in the tower above. It was weathered and hadn't seen paint during its lifetime. We could see both inside and out between the cracks of its siding. It did, however, offer an excellent view of the open fields and the wooded area facing our rifle and MG positions.

Lt. Collins, seldom without his runner, Jerry Ford, and a randomly selected squad of riflemen, ran daily reconnaissance patrols to within earshot, or often sight of the enemy lines, maintaining constant surveillance.

He never lost a man and managed a stealthy covert touch with the enemy without adding to our casualty rosters.

In spite of an impacted and infected molar, exhaustion,

a soaring fever and "walking" pneumonia, Collins was continually avoiding our assigned battalion aid man.

Finally the aid man smooth-talked the lieutenant into taking a GI "horse pill" and something else he tricked him into ingesting.

After two days of "no recall" he discovered he had been spirited away to an Evac hospital in Saverne, miles to the rear.

For the next two weeks he would find himself off the line for the only time during G Company's tour of combat. What all the kraut small arms, artillery and armored had attempted unsuccessfully was ironically accomplished by an assortment of microscopic bugs.

Again, this only compounded our company's immediate need for officer leadership. We were down to one.

After the lieutenant's evacuation to the Saverne Evac Hospital, his Third Platoon Sgt. Billy Culp took over the recon patrol leadership, and on two such assignments, one rifleman, Natividad Ranjel, was killed outright, three were wounded, and five were taken prisoner.

Under battalion orders Lt. Shepherd assigned Culp's patrols and would send runners out, pulling a man from each two-man hole until a sufficient number was reached for the task at hand. Almost daily the mortar section would receive a visit from Jerry Ford (Lt. Collin's runner), and Sgt. Schaeffer would pick a volunteer for patrol.

I was such a "volunteer" on one such occasion and, fortunately, the outcome did not bring about my anticipated demise and came off uneventfully.

The first incident left Ranjel dead. On another, Don Parish, George Steffell, Paul Pederzani, Tom Wilson and Jesse Teagarden were overwhelmed by a Jerry gun placement, and pinned down after running out of ammo were faced with sure death or surrender. They chose the latter. Sgt. Culp negotiated an escape for the balance of the patrol, which originally numbered twenty troops and returned with only fourteen.

The next day on a similar Culp led patrol, Tom Brant (third platoon second scout), as well as J.B. Lewis and Glenn Long, were each hit with bursts of burp gun fire. Sgt. Culp and the others of this smaller patrol, managed to get the wounded out and back the two to three hundred yards to the company lines and safety.

We occupied a thinly held line not more than two hundred yards from the enemy. They seemingly wanted none of us and we, by company command orders, similarly attempted to avoid any direct confrontation with them. The recon patrols were, to battalion command, apparently necessary. However, to the riflemen involved they were feared, hated, and despicable tasks that could only be the contrivances of some rear echelon brass.

Lt. Shepherd assumed company command and along with the residual company headquarters noncom staff took billets just off the company line.

Prior to his evacuation, Lt. Collins (aside from harassing both us and the enemy with his recon patrols), along with his recon patrols, along with Lt. Brunel Christensen (forward observer), called in enough of our available 105 firepower to make the Germans aware of our presence.

Our mortars were quiet at Koenigsbruck. I remember pulling observation at the grist mill OP; however, I don't recall our putting the 60mm mortars into action. We mortar guys were starting to feel more like footslogging riflemen.

One memorable moment, however, came as an apparent Allied fighter plane flew out of the horizon east of us and the enemy lines. It took a close pass at the grist mill, banked and then climbed out and away.

There were probably two of us on OP at the time, and Willie was with me. Anyway, the rickety wooden stairs, handrails and all, nearly gave way to our flight as we (not knowing if the plane was friend or foe) bolted down to the ground below in record time.

In Koenigsbruck, we Weapons guys did have the relative ease of rearguard positions and found the comfort of a small wood-floored cottage nestled against a canal that cut directly through the village. We slept on the floors, complained about slivers, and had the luxury of "fart sacks" and the warmth of a colorfully tiled stove. A far cry from the cold, damp holes the guys on the line a hundred yards away called home.

There was the continued intensity from the field artillery from both sides. However, the composition of the German combat team always seemed to provide an unfair balance of armored and supporting foot soldiers.

So it was in Koenigsbruck. When our troops went out on a combat patrol it was always riflemen with possibly the support of a light 30 machine guns (sans tripod) a grease gun, a BAR and occasionally a "ball" mortar; however, we had no armored support.

Not so with our adversaries. More often than not they rolled up with a Tiger and hammered us with eighty-eights. Rumors that the heavy stuff with which we were being harassed primarily came from these eighty-eight mounted Tigers were strengthened by the now familiar sounds of creaking drive sprockets and the clatter of tracks from somewhere past the nearby woodland.

Lt. Christensen aptly maintained better and even balance when he gave his fire orders to our 105 batteries.

The line soldiers fought off the numbing cold and

loneliness through sleepless days and nights. They pulled themselves deep into their holes when duty allowed. Their diggings were by necessity placed yards apart in order to cover the designated Company MLR.

A STRATEGIC WITHDRAWAL

ORDERS FROM SGT. Art Stuemke to his squad leaders to report to Lt. Shepherd at the Company CP were sent down the line by Ford, now serving as company runner for the lieutenant.

Sgt. Spearing was one of those squad leaders. Sgt. Martin and the other few remaining non-coms were given similar orders to report to company command.

When queried about his orders by Spearing, Ford shrugged off an answer with a short "I don't know," and with that Spearing headed for the snow-covered bunker which housed the CP.

Spearing was sure his platoon sergeant's orders would entail an exhausting third night in a row of manning a lonely company outpost and was not looking forward to that probability. However, there would be no "third night" of cold loneliness nor enemy, imaginary or real, for any of us that night.

Spearing's new orders were only a part of an overall action which included straightening the entire command's MLR and would take us ultimately past Haguenau and to Kaltenhouse and the Moder River.

Our entire company—originally numbering 182 at T.O. strength and now numbering less than half of that after the Gambsheim, Hatten-Rittershoffen conflicts—would be pulling out that evening.

Spearing was introduced to an engineer battalion officer, and along with Stuemke the three of them settled down in the bunker as the lieutenant spoke.

His message held an ominous tone and Spearing reflected to himself that for the first time in his recall, a lowly pair of sergeants and a shavetail lieutenant were made privy to the "Real Shit."

According to the lieutenant, the entire 7th Army was to secure a new line of defense with our positions to be along the south bank of the Moder River, and this entailed pulling back our particular position at least a full twenty kilometers. Between where we were, Koenigsbruck, and Haguenau were sprinkled units of the much renowned

10th and 21st SS Panzer Divisions, and the 25th Grenadiers along with additional Wehrmacht.

Spearing envisioned capture for the first time as a probability and felt his self-proclaimed luck was running low. His specific orders—given him while the lieutenant, Stuemke and he were sprawled out on their bellies on the straw-strewn bunker—were to assemble a detail of six riflemen at the Koenigsbruck School by 1700 hours that evening. At 2400 midnight they were to pull out, as a rearguard action, long after the rest of the company had left the area.

They were to follow a route through the woods and to the open highway which three times would cross bridges over the Sauer and the Eberbach rivers. Each of these bridges were, according to the lieutenant, held by our engineers and had been prepared for demolition. The lieutenant had scratched out the route of this rearguard action on a scrap of paper. This makeshift map was now entrusted to Spearing.

The engineers manning the bridges had instructions to hold their positions until the arrival of Spearing's rifle detail and assemble in Haguenau.

The lieutenant's words of praise for Spearing about his selection for the task at hand (with much ado about "secrecy") did little to aid the gripping feeling in his stomach and his sudden urge to crap. Thoughts of surviving the war suddenly became even more unreal and distant. As he often did, Spearing turned those down moments to thoughts of his wife and the young sons whom he missed so dreadfully. The uncanny luck which he so long had known as his protectorate had seemingly disappeared. Instead, he was in this unwanted place and in a position of unwanted and ultimate responsibility.

Obedience was not a blind response to command for the young sergeant. It was simply the thing you did, no more, no less, and by 1700 hours that evening he had rounded up his riddled squad—including Gall, Kent and King—and together they headed for the schoolhouse.

They settled down the best they could, discussed the chore at hand with the limited information Spearing had allowed, and waited for the evening to pass. They were now alone, as the rest of G Company was well out on the road to Haguenau. They searched for warmth within the walls of the schoolhouse while the cold winds began an unwelcome search across the schoolyard just outside. Midnight seemed forever away.

Weapons Platoon, including our mortar squad, was already on the road heading toward Haguenau along with the rest of the rifle troops of G Company. Sgt. Schaeffer had ordered us to assemble in front of the cottage we had called home for the past few days.

We stripped our gear to the bare minimum and prepared to evacuate, carrying only light field packs, trenching tools, carbines, M1s, and sidearms. Mortar tubes, base plates, gun sights, and machine guns had been loaded onto Richard Bertke's Jeep, and the ammo was loaded onto the ammo carrier towed behind Murry MacFee's Jeep.

The sun had just settled down below the houses along the canal that cut through the village. It added a beautiful, soft winter sunset to the already pristine village atmosphere.

We prepared to move out. The gear we intended to leave behind, including "fart sacks" and blankets, lie invitingly in an orderly fashion on the slivered wooden floor. The comfort this equipment had offered us would be most certainly missed.

The few rooms we shared had given "Weapons" our only indoor warmth over the past few days, and the only feeling of luxury for the past week and a half.

Spread out in a loose "column of twos" we proceeded south along the highway toward Haguenau with our section, including Willie and me, bringing up the company rear. The winds picked up a bit as we made our way down the road. As we labored along fighting what had become a very uncomfortable pace, more extraneous gear fell by the wayside.

First, gas masks, then shelter halves and trenching tools, then raincoats and finally, even overcoats pockmarked the light snow cover as we trudged along the way.

The winds picked up and cut through our clothing and only the sweat from within kept us somewhat warm. Those who had shed themselves of overcoats and rain gear now sorely missed them.

The road in front of us, now heavily traveled by preceding troops, jeeps and ammo carriers, became ice packed and two steps forward and one back became more commonplace. Some fell awkwardly as they slipped to the frozen macadam, their remaining gear rattling to the ground in an eerie expression of the night. The soles of their feet felt every bump of ice and stone under their shoepacs.

And now, those who had discarded their overcoats truly began to feel their loss as the chilling winds cut even deeper through the crisp air. The Haguenau evergreens bent all the more from their stern sentinel positions.

As the night moved on the more tired we became and orders for "take ten" every hour or so seemed only to come once in an eternity. This would undoubtedly become one of the longest nights in the memories of many of us who made that trek, and, perhaps even more so for those of

Spearing's rearguard action and the engineers they would pick up along the way.

G Company, now under the single command of Lt. Shepherd and a handful of noncoms, moved along a westerly direction through the Foret Dom de Koenigsbruck and North of Soufflenheim.

Travel was even more treacherous than that of a few hours before. The winds picked up and the night became even more abysmal.

Twice the column was stopped by intermittent parachute flares some far distance in front of us and barely visible over the horizon. So, twice more our troops dropped where they were, and crawled to the side of the road and crusted earth and thin layer of fresh snow. We waited there for the response of enemy mortars and/or artillery.

Nothing came, however, and the only interruption was the low rumble of cannon fire somewhere off in the distance. Ours... theirs... we didn't know, and we were nearly numbed into not caring.

Our two company vehicles pursued a leapfrog route in order to maintain contact with the rear of our beleaguered column. The drivers would pick up the ill and straggling, take them to the front of the column, drop them off and return for others.

On we went in a numbed and disjointed column, one

foot falling where another had left. Each troop struggled in keeping with his comrades, knowing that alone they would fail, but as a group they would succeed in reaching that Valhalla the brass called Haguenau.

REARGUARD ACTION

Sɢᴛ. Sᴘᴇᴀʀɪɴɢ ʜᴀᴅ carefully and repeatedly studied the map the engineer officer had entrusted to him, and he would continue to do so until their departure from the Koenigsbruck schoolhouse at midnight. He had considerable time to realize the extent of their mission.

Lives were at risk at their success or failure, and he knew full well that the engineers waiting for them at each of the bridges probably knew nothing of their planned escape route.

The first two bridges crossed the Sauer and were reached and blown by the engineers without difficulty. The engineers (not unlike Spearing's detail) were ready to run, non-stop if need be, all the way to Haguenau immediately upon completion of their mission, and, after each demolition they fell in with Spearing's ranks.

However, at the Eberbach bridge they hit a snag. The winds had whipped up to a frenzy. Sheets of ice, sleet and snow made it impossible to see but a few short feet ahead. They almost overran the waiting engineer's advance guard before he located them in the darkness, and in turn, led them to his section sergeant.

There was a problem, the sergeant told Spearing. The two officers in charge of the demolition had not finished wiring the bridge and that it would take some time to complete the job.

Spearing sent one of the engineers forward to the demolitions team leader, a captain, with the suggestion that he and his fellow officer should stay with their task and the others would move forward to the Haguenau side of the bridge and await the "Big Bang." The captain concurred and Spearing moved the remaining troops up.

The engineers, now a dozen or so, huddled around their one jeep and groused considerably about the need to wait. Impatient, and anxious to get going, one of them half-heartedly mumbled something about leaving the two officers to their heroics, and "splitting."

Finally, after a sudden flash and a horrific explosion ripped through the night, the two officers raced out from the firs. A feeling of relief spread through the ranks. The captain tendered his authority over to Spearing and his map with an anxious, "Let's get the hell outta here."

He told Spearing that he had "confiscated" and later admitted to having "flat stolen" the jeep from some line company. His people were in ill-health, and accordingly, needed to ride as often as possible—so the "stolen" or "confiscated" vehicle came to excellent use.

Spearing took his own crew to the lead, setting up a liaison of two engineers between his group, those engineers on foot, the two officers and the jeep idling along behind.

They made good time moving almost directly west and through a wooded area along a timber path identified by their map as Alle de Haslach. They were approaching the intersection of Alle de Mittelweg when the captain sent word forward requesting that they slow down for his weakened troops.

Shortly thereafter, the captain suggested that they had made a wrong turn. Spearing's map proved the officer wrong, however, and while the two of them pondered the situation under a raincoat with a flickering Zippo, the rest of their charges took a much needed break.

Hours and miles ahead, Lt. Shepherd, Sgt. Martin of weapons and second platoon's Sgt. Paine continued to lead their units in the forced march on through the night.

Again the column stopped. This time rumors of land mines ahead ran back through the ranks like the GI shits.

Soon the engineers had cleared the trail and after a welcome half hour to the side of the road we were again on our way. Some of us even caught a moment's sleep. Others managed cigarettes under their field jackets, raincoats or under whatever else they had to hide the lighter fire and cigarette glow. We had become real experts at hiding even the least flicker of light under cover of night. Our eyes burned. We choked, spit, hacked and coughed... but, we smoked.

When all seemed to be a never ending nightmare, and each attempt to rise after another fall to the ice glazed macadam and hard packed snow, Haguenau appeared and etched a welcome sight across the horizon.

Allied and Axis artillery units alike lightly touched the skies with alternating muzzle flash accompanied with the low rumble of their field batteries at work far off in the night. Shortly thereafter, a similar pattern of flickering light, slightly more brilliant and a little noisier, would be evidenced by the shell bursts from those same guns.

They lent an eerie feeling of distance between ourselves and the war at hand. Haguenau was such a welcome sight, and we wondered if the enemy truly did not know of our long march through the night.

As the buildings became more clearly defined we knew that some rest was at hand, but nothing so easy was to be our fate. Scattered farm buildings replaced closely spaced homes and then shops and workhouses became large factories, and on we went. One foot in front of the other… never ending… seldom resting.

The buildings now seemed to dissipate. They came fewer and farther apart and now an occasional farm house appeared. Had we been lied to? There was no stopping at Haguenau, there would be no warm billets for the night. No hot chow, and on we went, one forced step followed the other. We had made it to Haguenau. Where was our reward? Why had we continued on past the outskirts? Would this night ever end?

When all seemed lost and we were totally numbed by the cold, the column stopped and we dropped off to the roadside. We had turned sharply back to the south and east with the outskirts of the city only a memory and we were resting just alongside of an airport, the Aer d' Haguenau.

It was now about 0500 hours and a long time had passed since our last break. A solitary outbuilding stood invitingly at the slightly elevated ground to our right. At Sgt. Schaeffer's quipped command, "Fall out girls," our section took refuge in this twenty by twenty squared palace of wooden floors and welcome shelter.

With or without cover, huddled together, we dozed off, unaware of the clapboard walls to ward off the night's continued cold. We were fortunate. Others in our column dropped to the road where they stopped. They either fell to a numbed sleep or succumbed for the balance of the night to cold stupor. Some fell one on the other, unable to find the strength to move.

It had been little wonder that the enemy had been so unaware of our sojourn. It probably was not that they were so inept. The storm had more than likely been our greatest ally. Its misery had also been the enemy's wintry perdition and had probably saved our allied asses.

"Thompson … Willson…. Gets your asses up and spell guard." It must have been Schaeffer... or maybe Martin... or, maybe just a bad dream. That's it... just a bad dream. Neither myself nor Willie alongside of me, budged.

The snow was now beginning to bank along the roadside, and slowed both Spearing's tired troops and the engineers as they reached the open highway. They turned south for two or three kilometers to pick up the Soufflenheim-Haguenau Highway which went directly west into Haguenau.

Turning to the north would have taken them directly onto a route which those in Spearing's detail remembered only too well.

HATTEN FLASHBACK

SOME TWO WEEKS before, on January 5th, G Company—
then under the command of Sgt. Martin—had been taken
by six-by trucks along that same route and unloaded in
front of a gasthaus in the village of Niederbetschdorf, the
memorable jumping off spot for the Hatten-Rittershoffen
battle.

That village, Niederbetschdorf, was now only a couple
of kilometers up the road. Spearing certainly would have
pondered over those recent "Hatten" memories had he
known at that time of the tremendous number of casualties that would later be reported by both allied and enemy
commands.

The US 14th Armored Division alone, while in con-
sort with the Rainbow and the 79th, reported 104 dead,
899 wounded and another 112 missing the week of the

13th through the 20th, all as a result of armored and infantry engagements on those same fields that lay between Hatten and Rittershoffen. They reportedly lost 83 vehicles including 39 tanks at that time.

The civilian losses—mostly women, children and elderly from Rittershoffen and Hatten—included 126 fatalities.

Most casualties were inflicted by the big stuff. Eighty-eights, mortars and the big rail guns were our real enemy. To my knowledge very few of our company fatalities fell to rifle fire, snipers, burp guns, grenades, or machine gun fire.

Guys like Johnny Frasell, who had the back of his foot ripped away by with an enemy machine gun burst, would certainly argue that point, however.

Incidents of close combat were rare opposed to assaults by the "Big Stuff," and "hand to hand" combat was nearly mythical. I personally saw enemy soldiers at any logical distance within which I could fire my carbine on three occasions, and with one exception they were but fleeting moments.

In retrospect, every mortarman must reflect on the unseen damage to life, limb and material he must have inflicted during the war as the result of the rounds he personally felt slip through his fingers and into the mortar tube.

The extremely memorable moments of "my war" always return as though they were stop action frames in one helluva good movie. I always have the feeling of disbelief and even though I know the incidents as fact I somehow wonder at their veracity.

Of the twelve G Company troops who died at the Gambsheim-Landgraben Canal and at Hatten, all to the best of my knowledge were to eighty-eights, mortars, and perhaps, land mines.

I do recall small arms tracer fire going well over our heads early the morning we pushed out from the canal at Gambsheim, and, later that afternoon being pinned down with automatic machine pistol fire while holding a finger of woods later that afternoon. But again, I have no recall of casualties from those same small arms.

The overhead tracer fire was, however, an enemy ploy to give us a feeling of security and develop our exposure to their well-defined machine gun fire at our actual level.

Leaving Rittershoffen we had taken considerable Tiger eighty-eight fire from Panzer units stationed between Oberroedern to the north and Hatten. Hatten was occupied by a mix of civilians and enemy soldiers, German panzer crews and grenadiers.

Our 105s and seventy-fives pounded the west end of the village, and with elements of the 14th Armored

Artillery and the 79th Infantry Division, the Germans were softened up and driven deeper into the hamlet. Task Force Wahl, as the operation came to be known, was now indeed operational.

Ultimately, the Fuhrer had personally demanded that Haguenau be taken and ordered the elimination of all allied combatants between the lower Vosges Mountains and the Rhine River.

First, however, they would have to penetrate the allied MLR at Hatten and Rittershoffen and to this end on the 9th of January Der Fuhrer committed the 25th Panzer Grenadiers, the 21st SS Panzer Division, the 47th Yolks Grenadiers, and the 7th Parachute Division.

There, the Germans additionally deployed four tank battalions, two Panzer recon battalions, five artillery battalions and an anti-tank battalion, all to the task of breaking through at Hatten-Rittershoffen.

In that assault on Hatten four days earlier, Sgt. Martin had smartly led us off the road as we left Rittershoffen.

He took us south of and parallel to the main road and through low snow banks fresh from several inches of new snowfall. Here we were much less the conspicuous target we had been while traipsing down the center of the road.

As we neared the west end of Hatten we came under the attack of three eighty-eight mounted Tiger tanks and a

Hatten, 1945

single halftrack. Our Third Rifle Platoon was to the north side of the road and made contact with our battalion commander, Major Norman G. Reynolds. Antitank support and artillery were soon on the way.

Willie and I watched in full view as a light American tank destroyer matched stride for stride and shell for shell with a German half-track. The churning tracks of both vehicles threw up trails of blackened snow as they sped across the open field not twenty yards apart. The TD's

75 mm cannon proved too much for the halftrack's heavy machine guns and stopped it in its tracks.

The German crew poured out and disappeared into ditches, drawing fire from some of the rifle troops who, along with the triumphant TD, brought about their demise.

With our artillery having now softened the enemy's positions and forcing their retreat further into the village, the initial entry into the town became less eventful. Our platoon managed to secure the first three or four houses and outbuildings to the left side of the road.

As our combined troops came in, most of the krauts and civilians pulled out in front of us. However, one unfortunate grenadier—apparently serving as an artillery observer—was taken prisoner as we entered town and was made to stand in the street as both our artillery and that of the enemy poured in.

Sgt. Martin settled us in shortly after we had cleared the first two houses on an alley that led directly north and out of town. It was late evening and the moon was full. Fresh snow covered everything and any evidence of our late afternoon struggle was hidden under a fresh blanket of white. The artillery from both sides subsided.

It was here and now that the "Big Stuff-Little Stuff" scenario seemed to fall apart for at least two of us.

Our section sergeant, Phil Schaeffer, and I pulled first guard that night and took positions in the northeast corner bedroom of the first house on the alley running north out of town. Most of the house was still standing, although its roof was partially ripped off.

The bedroom was empty other than a broken wooden bed frame, a torn and frayed feather tick lying in the corner, with debris scattered everywhere.

Sgt. Schaeffer immediately curled up in the corner with the blanket, volunteered my services for the first watch and attempted some shut eye. I propped myself up against the bed frame, threw a magazine of 30 caliber in my carbine, peered out through the window down the alley and prepared for a long two hour's watch.

It was an unusually quiet winter's night. Fresh snow, clear skies and the moon shone as brightly as a stadium floodlight. Everything was crisp, clear and clean. I nodded lightly, fighting fatigue and a lack of any recent deep sleep.

My head fell and my chin struck my chest. The added weight of my helmet slowed the jerking motion of my head as it snapped back to attention.

Again my chin dropped and my eyelids fell, and again, I felt myself drifting off only to jerk my head back, my eyes straining to maintain vision of the alley ahead.

I was suddenly jolted into wide-eyed reality as I looked up the alley. Several German soldiers approached at slung arms. Bandoleers of ammunition were strapped across their chests over white snow capes.

Heads down, two abreast in a staggered informal line they walked up the alley, and ironically, past the first house occupied by our troops, and approached our post. They apparently knew no more of our position than we had known of theirs.

"Halt... Hande hoak," I managed in my best kraut. the line stopped and after a slight pause they all dispersed. One peeled off and sped across the alley. I let one round fly as I shouldered my carbine and he disappeared behind the building on the far side of the alley. I thought I saw him spin as though hit.

Another streaked up the alley toward the main road, straight past me and by the outside bedroom wall.

"Don't shoot they're Americans!" someone yelled out from the building next door. "Americans my ass!!" I retorted, now joined by a wide-eyed and extremely wide awake Sgt. Schaeffer.

Two more of the shocked enemy detail had turned and had run straight back to the orchard from where they had first appeared. Two others hit the snow in back of a low shrub not more than ten feet in front of Schaeffer and me.

I sat on the open sill and emptied the rest of the magazine into the shrubs.

I attempted to slip another magazine into the chamber. I trembled. A surge of excitement raced through me. My hands shook and the magazine slipped past my carbine, out of my hands, off the window sill and fell harmlessly to the snow below. By hanging precariously from the sill I recovered the magazine and managed to load it into my rifle while Sgt. Schaeffer assumed my post at the window.

We watched for long moments for movement from the shrubs, but none came. My thoughts were becoming more perceptive and I had vivid recall of potato mashers sticking out from the kraut bandoleers and snow capes. We were an easy lob away.

While Schaeffer covered me from the window, I went out the side door and positioned myself at the southwest outside corner of the cottage. I had a good clear view of two shadowed forms lying very still a short distance from the shrub where they had taken refuge.

Long moments passed before I made out some movement as one of the sinister forms slowly backed off toward the orchard. The other lay very still. The full moon and the fresh snow continued to provide near daylike vision. I took careful aim, fired and the body jumped as the bullet found its target.

Again time seemed to stand still, and again the quiet filled the night. I watched horrified as the dark figure moved once again and dragged slowly across the snow. God, why didn't he lay still? Once more I drew my carbine to my shoulder. My vision blurred. My finger weakened as it squeezed at the trigger. There was no excitement now. Shame... fear... compassion, weakness maybe… but, certainly no excitement.

That dark evil form was quiet once again. I lowered my gun and after agonizing moments the dreaded movement returned. I was through… and I... the cowboy... the hero felt a little bit sick. I watched as he moved back through the snow, slowly closing the distance between himself and the porched house across the way.

Neither Schaeffer nor I spoke as we returned to the beet cellar in search of guard relief. We each knew in our heart of hearts that he would make it.

In spite of the comforts and protection of a beet cellar there was little rest and no sleep for the rest of that night. There was an inordinate amount of prayer, however.

The next morning I heard reports of a snow covered body that lay outside at the foot of a shrub.

Another reported that a young German soldier—blond and about sixteen—had been found on a porch. He was bleeding badly, but alive. He was bandaged by our medics, tossed onto Steve Markovitz's weapons Jeep and taken to a field hospital somewhere to the rear.

The following day I found that I couldn't...wouldn't... and didn't want to look out into that yard. I wasn't sure what was there and wasn't going to find out.

Ironically, the next day Steve Markovitz was killed in that same house. He had been preparing a cup of Nescafe in his canteen cup when a single mortar blast tore through a window and a partial wall and left a tail fin assembly buried between his shoulder blades. He just, turned, took a deep gasp, fell through the doorway into a hallway and crumpled to the floor. His body lay there most of the day.

I don't believe I saw him fall. Art Pethybridge did and could never forget. I'm sure I was in the beet cellar when it happened, yet, strange as it may seem, the only way I remember Markovitz was standing over a tiled stove sipping Nescafe from a blackened aluminum cup. He was a heavy set, broad shouldered, wavy-haired hulk of a guy and full of life, and probably the biggest man in our company. He seemed strangely larger in life than in death.

ANOTHER BRIDGE
TO BLOW

Now, some two weeks later, we found ourselves just a few kilometers away on this "must do" mission intent on providing some credibility to our allied lines.

Spearing, his rearguard detail and the group of engineer add-ons continued to trudge along. Some small farm homes dotted the horizon and they proceeded, ever nearer to their destination. They were now just some eight or nine kilometers from Haguenau, "hot chow" and a much needed rest.

Early morning approached, came and went. The troops were all "beat" and at the engineer officer's suggestion they slowed their pace. They took an "extra" ten now and then to compensate for the engineers' lack of foot soldier stamina. The jeep was God sent.

Soon the sun was burning off the wintry haze and blue skies prevailed. The winter storm and its diabolic protection against the enemy had disappeared.

New barriers against the Spearing mission's successful completion presented themselves. The Luftwaffe was noted for daylight surveillance and individual sorties along the open highways searching out convoys and the like.

Enemy foot soldiers often holed up in the outlying farm communities in support of artillery and panzer units lying in wait with their eighty-eights poised for action.

And, there was always the possibility of a spotter, hiding furtively, watching for stray allied troops to be targeted for Haguenau Hattie and her thunderous response. The possibility of our salient pulling back through this "no man's land" without tremendous losses was nil, even with the cover of a winter storm. But now, with the storm lifting, the daylight and bright skies made it even more implausible.

As morning passed the sun now shone even more brightly. The sky was a perfect blue, and the temperature continued to drop. Spearing now could see his entire procession.

Vapor trails formed from their labored breathing as they struggled against the cold. Several inches of new snow lay across the highway and drifted over the gutters and up its banks. It weighted down the boughs of the tall firs to the right. Open fields lay to the left.

There was absolutely no evidence of the large number of our troops as well as those of several German units that had passed over the highway just days before. In the case of our own company command, it was just hours before. This same route had been used by the Seventy-Ninth when it had given way to the men of Love Company, Third Battalion some three weeks prior. Love Company used the same route when they moved back to Haguenau after we had replaced them at Koenigsbruck.

It was obvious that the German Panzer units had created a lot of stress with their hit and run tactics throughout the area. Now, the fresh snow hid all of this prior disruption and the cold, white silence seemed to belie the entire war.

The engineer officer who had originally assigned Spearing his mission either failed to tell him of yet another bridge (a fourth)—or perhaps he had just not known of one. However, a fourth and last bridge did appear as they approached yet another river crossing. Here it formed a deep and insurmountable gorge some few hundred yards north of the intersection of the two main highways.

King was the first to spot trouble as they neared the

bridge: a single troop holding down a slit trench not fifty yards away. Not knowing whether this soldier was friend or foe, Spearing ordered his detail to lay back while he and King made contact. Much to their relief, an even more relieved GI ran back to meet them, his hand outstretched in a warm welcome. His orders were to await the arrival of any late retreating troops until dawn and no later. The bridge was loaded with charges sufficient to blow it completely out of the Haguenau Forest. Fortunately, he had waited nearly an hour past dawn.

With the bridge intact there had been a retreat route for foot soldiers, vehicles and the remaining Allied Forces. However, with the bridge gone, the gorge made even an infantry retreat nearly impossible. Spearing realized how close they had come to losing the use of their jeep, and even more importantly, the inability of the engineers to move anywhere without it.

When no troops had shown, the lone sentinel had determined to wait with his hand ready and remaining on the detonator. As fate would have it, he happened to look back one last time and spotted Spearing's crew coming through.

With his hand poised he had waited, and only after he spotted the jeep, was he sure of their identity and realized that they were GIs in retreat and not Germans intent on attacking his position.

Spearing took his small force across the bridge and the lone engineer went about his job without delay. The blast thundered up the river gorge ominously and after but a few moments waiting for an enemy response they gathered together, entered the Soufflenheim-Haguenau Autobahn and headed west and straight into Haguenau.

A mile or so prior to arriving at the Haguenau outskirts, a white caped figure darted across the road some fifty yards in front of them. Spearing's crew hit the ditches and at almost that same moment King spotted an American tank in support of a group of engineers laying mines on that same road. Neither detail paid heed to the other as Spearing's group passed by and the caped figure had disappeared uneventfully.

King worked his way over to the side of his sergeant and urged him to look to the approaching Haguenau skyline with a foreboding premonition that it probably wouldn't be there in a few days.

The only other incident of note that preceded their entry into Haguenau and on to Kaltenhouse, other than the continued cold and stone bruised feet, was an encounter with some disoriented civilians who were heading directly into what Spearing had determined must be the enemy lines. Spearing's detail turned them about, probably fifteen in all, and they streamed off toward Haguenau ahead of the troops.

The young soldier pondered at the "noise" some had made stateside about fighting on foreign soil. He quietly thanked God that his wife and children were not among those in that refugee group and were safe some 3000 miles across the sea.

KALTENHOUSE SECURED

EARLY THAT SAME morning, on January 21ˢᵗ, Sgt. Schaeffer mustered his mortarmen just outside the airport line shack. We were none too fresh from but two hours sleep and there was still very vivid recall of the prior night's vigil of fifteen or more miles of forced marching.

Our rise before daybreak and the cold crisp air did nothing to dispel our aches and pains, nor defuse an inordinate amount of grumbling.

Pulling ourselves together with renewed promises from our sergeant of some "hot chow," we fell in in back of Sgt. George Snow's First Platoon and Art Stuemke's Third Platoon and stumbled off down the highway skirting Haguenau and headed southwest past the airport and on toward Kaltenhouse.

The hot chow never came. "K" rations would, again,

be the fare of the day. The grumbling became more vociferous and nasty as we plodded along, wondering if this day was to be anything like the last.

Sgt. Phil Schaeffer, dispersed our ranks in an "as skirmishers" formation as we approached Kaltenhouse in anticipation of rumored resistance.

As we entered Kaltenhouse, Willie and I remained cautiously separated by several yards. We took to the center of the road searching diligently above to the left and right.

A single shot rang out and popped over our heads as it smacked into the slope beyond. We hit the ground and a trio more shots cracked over us. It was obviously sniper fire from one of the many scattered buildings which lined each side of the road.

We continued to search upward for the source of our harassment, anticipating another shot and, perhaps, the sight of a rifle muzzle blast. None came, and moments later we were ordered to do a search.

Willie and I moved along a retaining wall to the right, crossed over the roadway and approached the nearest building to our left. It was a large lofted wood frame barn. There was a small bell room like structure at the crown of its roof and it appeared threateningly as an ideal spot for a sniper. Willie hit the ground along the right side. I followed close behind and slid up along his side.

While I provided cover, "buddy style," Willie scrambled to the huge wooden doors and threw the closest open.

While he covered, I went through the doorway and dropped to the dirt inside. The building was open and appeared totally vacated. However, straw from the loft above caught my eye and I either saw or imagined movement from above.

A rickety appearing ladder was propped, not too invitingly to me, against the header reaching the loft above. Gathering all of my "cowboy" courage, with my buddy Willie covering me, I more than cautiously climbed the ladder. I poked the barrel of my carbine into the straw ahead of me as I went. As I approached the top I crawled deeper into my helmet, waiting for "whatever" to explode in my face.

After making one last thrust forward with my rifle, I dropped one foot down in search of a rung and all hell broke loose. Straw flew in every direction and I went sprawling backwards "ass over teacup" to the ground some eight feet below.

A triumphant hen fluttered over me and settled to the ground nearby, squawking as she went. Even Willie was too startled to see the immediate humor in my predicament. The score: Indians 1, Cowboys 0.

Neither spoke of our heroics. Sgt. Schaeffer would

never find out, nor would our buddies. Out on the road again we sheepishly watched Lt. Shepherd, Sgt. Graham and our company runner move out to determine our positions, and finally our MLR was set.

Our machine guns covered a large area from the extreme left flank to a second gun some one hundred yards to the right and adjacent to the rifle platoons covering the center. Our light mortars were dug in slightly to the rear, and the CP close to the right flank.

Our forward observation was to be positioned at the far end of a village lane, the Rue des Pêcheurs. This lane ran directly down from the main road that skirted Kaltenhouse to the Moder River's south bank.

Six farmhouses sat on the sides of this road, the last two of which actually rested close to the river bank. From either of these there was a direct line of sight to the wooded area that lay at the north side of the river and extended back to Camp Oberhoffen.

A "SHITTY" SITUATION

SGT. PAINE WAS originally assigned the sector between the airfield and the Moder by Lt. Shepherd. This was a memorable event to the young sergeant as he was attempting the privacy of personal latrine duty when the lieutenant searched him out to relay those orders.

They found an area just past a series of convoluted ridges, each one some eight to ten feet in height. Here the topography leveled off and offered an almost ideal view of the river.

Needless to say, the gasses in the sergeant's lower bowel continued to build up to untowardly high pressure while all this maneuvering was going on. Had the lieutenant been so inclined he would have noticed the sergeant's discomfort by the manner of his walk.

When the lieutenant continued about his chores of

securing the other rifle platoons the sergeant beat a quick retreat for the nearest lower level. Hurriedly he tore away at layers of combat uniform, first his outer pants, then combat pants, wool pants and finally his long johns. Cold numb fingers and relaxed guard when preparing to squat brought about a "shitty" situation.

By the time he had "dry cleaned" with shreds of long johns torn away by his bayonet, orders had been changed and the sergeant along with his charges were sent off to Kaltenhouse. Someone else inherited his latrine and the surrounding area, which was later overrun by the Germans and its new occupants pushed back into the airfield.

The First and Third Platoons and the machine gun section went in first, followed by Paine some distance in front of his men, searching out the area as he went. Ordered to "straddle" the road he positioned squads in three or four timber and plaster houses on the left side of the road.

He set up his platoon CP on the right side with a BAR on each side facing back toward Haguenau. Only stray sniper fire interrupted G Company's initial entry into the village, and within the hour guns were in place and everything was secure. It seemed, other than Willie's and my encounter with the barn fowl, like a piece of cake.

CAMP OBERHOFFEN

FROM OUR LEFT flank we faced two hundred yards of snow covered meadow. It was strung with rolls of barbed concertina wire from the frontage road to the paralleling Moder River and on to the enemy stronghold, Camp Oberhoffen.

The camp was some six hundred yards from our lines at this point and was hidden by a heavily wooded outgrowth of evergreens. This area was overrun with German foot soldiers, light armored vehicles, machine gun nests and, worst of all, their forward artillery observers.

Oberhoffen itself was about four miles square with general quarters as large as the entire village of Kaltenhouse.

Cousins to the gigantic German railguns that had continually let us know of their ominous presence were said to be hiding within the camp itself. Sgt. Graham assured us that the low cranking rumble we heard was from these magnificent giants rolling out to fire, recoiling and then squeaking back into position after spewing out their thunder on some unknown allied target off in the distance.

Our exposed center ran even closer to the river bank and as it closed from our positions from left to right. Our right flank was our most forward outpost and, was the closest position to the enemy and Oberhoffen. Here the Rue des Pêcheurs and "Fish Street" met the Moder River.

The main road, skirting the village which we used as our primary line of defense, moved directly east from our point of entry. After perhaps two hundred and fifty yards or so it arched back some thirty degrees at an oblique angle to the southeast. It continued from there for another two hundred yards where another road dead ended into it at a right angle. Here G Company and the battalion positions ended as did the outskirts of the village.

The main road continued on in a straight southeasterly line and out of town for another hundred and fifty yards where it took a sharp ninety-degrees directly up and into the southwest gate of Oberhoffen. This latter area was in full sight of the camp itself and was zeroed in by their artillery and mortars. It would have been strategically suicidal to attempt to either defend or attack.

On more than one occasion while we defended Kaltenhouse, the enemy offered a halftrack, ground transport or some other armored vehicle as a target by running this same route directly into Kaltenhouse and our positions.

Often a Tiger tank would make its way toward the center of our lines just falling short of entering the town itself. Also, the German's Oberhoffen artillery was well targeted on our positions along the open road.

A WELL DEFINED TARGET

THE DEFENSE OF Kaltenhouse was one of "spreading the troops" and the platoon sergeants were faced with quite a chore in achieving this goal.

Single squads would be dug in along the roadway so sparsely that holes and trenches were barely visible one from the other. With no communications lines in, the Platoon Sergeants and their guides were the primary link between posts and were constantly touring their commands.

On one occasion the intrepid Sgt. Paine, while checking his squad positions, passed by both machine gun positions and the Company CP.

He had proceeded halfway to the village center and was working his way along a retaining wall that rose above the roadway in full view of the Germans.

The quiet was broken with the sudden, yet familiar

scream and following after blast of an eighty-eight shell as it tore into the ground and exploded but a few feet away. He hit the ground and lay still, having nothing more than an M1 to face the heavy armor and/or artillery—which ever it may have been.

After a few harrowed moments he managed a return to back to his CP, only to find that he was not welcomed by his platoon members. It seemed that wherever he went he found enemy fire.

If Jerry decided on lobbing in mortars, Paine's movements coincided with leaving the comforts of a building or house for a trip to the CP. If he occasioned to make an inspection of platoon positions, the krauts would decide on an eighty-eight barrage.

His reputation had become such that his platoon runners decided that he should make his rounds alone. Caught in such a discussion of being "through" going out with the sergeant, Platoon Runner "Handle Bar" Bill Henry was told that he "would" assume such duty; however, he would also be given the opportunity of closely auditing the alternating procedure with the other runners.

The sergeant had not realized until this episodical revelation that things were relatively quiet and that it was he who was getting all the enemy's attention.

Haguenau Hattie lent credence to his reputation. I

remember Hattie as having fired but four times on our positions in Kaltenhouse. One of these shells left a crater twelve feet across and four feet deep in back of our mortar gun placements. The others, naturally, found Sgt. Paine and all but destroyed two houses which he had just recently vacated.

DIGGING IN

SGT. SCHAEFFER LOCATED a trio of cottages in our section's assigned area. One nestled slightly in back of another and adjacent to a third which could provide logical defilade for our mortar placements.

Shortly thereafter, our guns were dug in—one hole, two guns—just two steps and a headfirst dive through the door of our kitchen CP or the beet cellar next door. Ammo was taken off the ammo carrier and laid aside the gun placements.

Mortar sergeants Ray Ruble and Lloyd Teale moved up to the furthest rifle outpost at the end of the Rue des Pêcheurs, located what they determined to be a reasonable general target, and returned to the mortar gun placements. No telephone lines were in and as a result they fired the first three rounds for effect..."by guess and by golly."

The mortar section with its numbers having been reduced to less than ten men, consolidated its strength to this one position and its two sixties with Ruble, Teale and Bill Nickeson sharing a "one squad" command. We were ready to go to work.

RUE DES PÊCHEURS

A TOTALLY FATIGUED, but also totally relieved Spearing and his detail plodded into the company area almost by accident. They felt that surely there would be a reward of chow and slumber immediately upon their contact with friendly lines.

The engineers had returned to their command in Haguenau and were back to doing their engineering. Spearing and his squad of King, Gall and Kent had stumbled into what they hoped to be at least our battalion area.

There they were spotted by Lt. Shepherd, who had just returned from inside Kaltenhouse on his mission of deploying his troops to their positions.

In his very uniquely unmilitary manner and with his low southern drawl he expounded on his surprise at "evah seein' yew agin." However, he could offer no food nor lodging... just an offer for an eventual break in a line shack at the Haguenau airport. It was probably the same shack that Willie and I had shared with some twenty other G troops earlier that same morning.

The lieutenant returned within the hour and led Spearing's squad—including himself, King, Gall, and Kent—across the snow deep into Kaltenhouse and a blacksmith's barn. They were joined later by Hawkins and Frasell, who rounded out his squad. In the meantime they raided a nearby hen house, and collected some eggs which they boiled with a few potatoes in Spearing's helmet over the blacksmith's bellows.

Their bellies temporarily satisfied, they made an in detail search of all six houses on the Rue des Pêcheurs, not fully realizing at that time they were to be, beyond a doubt, the forward outpost for G Company.

They determined that the most logical house in which they should hole up would be the first one on the right going down the hill to the Moder. There they could best defend the company positions should the Germans make an attempt to break through their defenses at that particular spot.

With two of them on duty the other four attempted some sleep. Their line of sight gave them full view of both sides and out to the enemy side of the Moder, its north bank rising to a snowy meadow that disappeared into a fir lined ridge no more than a hundred yards away.

FARMING KALTENOUSE

ALL THE BARNS, outbuildings and yards were overrun with cattle. Some were locked in the barns and assumed to be safe and out of harm's way. There were hutches for the rabbits and shacks for the geese. Vegetables were found in each of the shallow cellars throughout the village. Arkansas Bob King prepared either boiled goose or rabbit stew.

Clint Murphy milked the cows and became the dairyman. Bill Nickeson peeled apples and stole all the "K" ration sugar in preparation of establishing his applesauce franchise. He damned near came to blows with Teale after being caught pillaging the fiery Teale's "K" ration sugar supply.

Eggs, once plentiful, were soon to become a premium. The more the eighty-eight's slammed home the more the surviving chickens and geese became traumatized. The more traumatized they became the less eggs were laid.

A beet cellar conversation overheard by Bill Nickeson and being related by George Atkins, a "good ol' boy" from southern Illinois went like this: "What ya gotta do is get thur legs up on the table an git at'em from behin'."

It took a while for Nickeson to realize the subject of Atkins distortion. It was definitely milking goats and not "nailin'" women.

Goat milk was plentiful until those same goats went dry. A couple of days passed before Atkins informed the rest of us that it was they—the goats and not we—who had to be watered. It was these same barnyard animals who gave so much to us when we had so little, both in sustenance and in purpose, who took the heaviest losses when the high explosives, including the eighty-eights and mortars, rained in.

With each barrage of artillery we hit the cellars or crawled more deeply into our bunkers. Not the poor "dumb" animals. They had no knowledge of what an overhead burst could do and knew nothing of phosphorous and time fire.

They just squawked… and… bellowed… fluttered and screeched, or, like the silent goats, they just ran. At least they ran until an artillery shell tore into their feathers or flesh.

THE ANIMALS

THESE HAPLESS CREATURES offered sad moments to all of us, however, this was especially true of guys like Bob King. An Arkansas farm boy, he understood the plight of the barnyard denizens. He chased after the smaller animals, the half dead and half alive, hoping to put them out of their misery.

A wounded cow fell through the outside entry of an open beet cellar and crazily struggled to get past its occupants, with Sgt. Paine going in and a startled mortar gunner going out. The gunner fired four shots directly into the animal's thick hard skull, the first three glancing off before the last penetrated home and the animal went down.

I remember only too well a later incident at Gélacourt when our outfit was back off the line for R & R. Some of our guys had been dynamiting for fish with grenades when I happened by.

I heard a low pathetic cry, almost like a baby, coming from a barn off to the left. I walked in and after slowly scanning across the open I spotted a small black cat, near kitten-size, cowering in the corner its ears pulled back tight to its head, teeth exposed and spitting.

Its hind legs, soaked blood red, hung loosely to the rear. I was carrying a forty-five I had picked up from one of our derailed gunners, and hoping to put the poor thing to an easier end, I drew careful aim at its head at no more than ten feet and squeezed off a round.

The cat went straight up, clawing out with its good front legs as it went. It came down running in a great circle about the barn, dragging its rear legs behind, spitting and spewing as it went. The hair stiffened at the back of my neck.

I found a wooden harvest rake propped up against the wall and after considerable effort I pinned the kitten to the ground and managed to dispatch it with one more round.

I had seen buddies fall and had taken considerable fire myself, but that terrible moment took its toll and is still deeply imbedded in my memory. The animals, not unlike the children, truly were the undeserving victims of war.

THE BIG STUFF

OUR FIRST SHELLING at Kaltenhouse came to me as almost a surprise. We had been so busy about putting things in order, and digging in, that the interruption came as a shock. As usual it was sheer devastation and actually came shortly after we had finished digging in our guns.

It came in salvos of three, probably Camp Oberhoffen field pieces, each triple on a predetermined and different target, and each incident separated minutes from the other.

The third or fourth volley came down on our mortar positions and the surrounding area. By now we were securely in our potato cellars and received no direct hit to the house we now called home. However, the house in front of us was leveled as was most of the one serving as defilade for our guns.

Almost immediately Sgt. Ray Ruble, one of the more cool heads in our command when it came time to man a mortar, crawled out to the guns, made a couple of sight adjustments to one, and, one after the other dropped every prepped round we had into the tube. As he crawled back into the cellar he turned to Ray Schumacher.

"That ought to teach the bastards... I gave 'em charge four!!!"

The shelling continued, often for a half hour or so before letting up. Plaster and timber flew, and only wood frames remained. Thatched roofs were blown away and the animals bellowed, squawked and squealed. Then it would become quiet and the blood chilling, eerie call "Medic... Medic," penetrated what had become near silence.

Hours might pass before the nightmarish fire returned and each time we would pull ourselves further down into the vegetable bins and slit trenches we used as an attempt to escape.

It was not unlike that same ice cold fear that came over us while awaiting more eighty-eights on the Landgraben Canal, and trying to cut through the ice crusted soil with nothing but our helmets for trenching tools. I'll never forget that wretched scratching sound as it penetrated the night.

However, they always returned. Sometimes, we were

forewarned with the sucking sound of their forward mortars as the shells left their tubes. Or sometimes we were warned by the piercing scream of their split nosed mortars as they found their targets nearby: a nerve shattering tactic of German warfare.

Mortars, other than split nosed, were unusually silent when they came in and their victims often "never knew what hit them."

Relief surged through one's body when the eighty-eight's shells fell short, tore at the earth harmlessly, or just shrieked on past.

This relief was, however, short-lived and too often replaced with an unusually long wait for more to come. Each of us had been lifted from the ground or thrown from a bunker as an enemy shell tore up our immediate area. We knew that ninety percent of all infantry casualties were the result of the heavy stuff and not small arms fire.

We, each in our own way, thanked our God every time we escaped unscathed, knowing that the odds for a foot soldier's survival were very thin.

We each fantasized about a "million dollar" dream wound that would take us off the line and send us home, hopefully none too much the worse for wear, leaving us totally whole, and especially with our "family jewels" in place.

THE MILLION DOLLAR WOUND

I RECEIVED MY Million Dollar Wound just two months after Kaltenhouse on a sloping hillside just outside Eunet, France. It was the second day of our "Big Push," March 16, 1945, and we had headed toward the Maginot.

We had successfully cut a huge salient over, and deep into the Vosges mountains. An eighty-eight mounted Tiger tank had pinned our rifle troops down and its shells were clipping down through the firs on the forward slope of the hill.

Boughs snapped, and snow, twigs and fir needles filled the air. I remember, turning as I fell, and looking right into the face of the blast as it smacked a fir some twelve feet below. Our squad was at full five-man T.O. strength following our reorganization at Gélacourt and that shell got three of us, including two replacements (who I never really got to know) and me.

Bill Nickeson, my squad leader at the time, and my buddy, Willie, stayed with me till the medics came. My wounds were not critical, but I was bleeding profusely and suffering severely from the result of shock.

Both Nick and Willie assured me that I had received that "million dollar" wound and insisted that I would be stateside within the week. It was more like a "$500,000 wound" as I didn't go straight home, however, I was out of action and away from all the "Bad Shit."

I lost consciousness several times only coming to later that night in an unguarded gravel pit at the foot of the hill. Apparently I had been deposited there by the medics.

Some two days later—with only glimpses at reality and nearly dead from loss of blood—I found myself on a litter in an open field hospital apparently far from our battalion lines.

I had been picked up by German troops, who were probably intent on surrendering. I was carried on a make-shift litter of rifles and a field jacket, jostled about for I don't know how long and finally left at the American lines, some-time, some place later. I returned to company duty just a little over two months later with the war pretty much over.

KIA

A BESPECTACLED MACHINE gunner, Wayne Scott, was the first of our troops to make the casualty roster on the morning reports in Kaltenhouse. "KIA" is the shortest final statement to relate the totality of a young man's life. Scotty was a quiet, do the job sort of a guy. He never had much to say and was somewhat different than the stereotype "don't give a shit" machine gunner.

News of his going down took no time at all to spread throughout the command. Word reached the mortar section immediately though we had no telephone lines out. The news of a fallen comrade was destined to move fast throughout the company, and especially true of Scotty. He had been with us at Gruber, and had shared the landing at Marseilles and CPII.

The shell, apparently an Oberhoffen eighty-eight, hit

both Scotty and the light thirty he was manning, tearing up his left shoulder and chest. Both gun and gunner were tossed out of the bunker.

Glenn Martin, a fellow MG gunner, got to Scotty first. Jake Shenefield, his section sergeant, arrived shortly after.

Bill Kenny, another gunner, worked his way across the exposed field between their two guns and reached Scotty just before he died. None of these close comrades could help him and he died in Glenn's arms a few short moments later.

Other G Company troops to die in defense of their country were Bert Hanson, Earnest Lee, Steve Markovitz, Hans Melzer, Joseph "Pat" Patterson, Natividad Ranjel, William Rosolie, Tom Sandridge, Paul Siegrist, Harley Stands, Bernard Smith, George Stoffel, Nathan Tallent, Pasquale Murno, Henry Strine, Donald Martin, and Louis Sutter. One in ten of those who shipped over together fell.

Those to die later as a result of wounds or as an aftermath of the war were Bill Hunnicutt, Tom Tewell, Lt. Shepherd, and Tom Dowling who was killed in the Korean conflict. They were twenty two in all.

DEFENDING KALTENHOUSE

F COMPANY HAD arrived in Kaltenhouse simultaneously with our arrival and, unfortunately, they were immediately dispatched across the open meadow to take up permanent positions along the roadway just to the northwest.

Moments after they left our Company area a horrendous barrage of enemy artillery rained down on the meadow. Sgt. Graham's recall was one of wonderment that any survived.

With F Company having moved out there was literally no longer a Second Battalion Front at Kaltenhouse itself. G Company would cover a front of roadway expanding over 800 yards with a like amount on the south bank of the Moder River.

This was an immense job for one line officer, a handful of non-coms and less than eighty other enlisted men. Camp Oberhoffen itself with its unknown numbers lie just a few hundred yards away.

Its "Champ de tir de maneuvers" spread out forebodingly over several square miles. None of us, including the officers and men of our immediate command, seemed to know at that time of its importance or of its compelling size.

Gambsheim, Hatten and Rittershoffen had diminished the company from a T.O. strength of 182 enlisted men and officers to its current pitifully weakened numbers of but one line officer and perhaps eighty enlisted men.

Privates had assumed squad leadership and staff sergeants had replaced lieutenants as platoon leaders. This was the company command that was to defend Kaltenhouse.

Earlier the same month the canal banks of Gambsheim claimed four second platoon troops with one shell burst. Many others fell during the first night out and our "indoctrination to fire" had been swift and complete.

The First and Third Platoons and our makeshift machine gun section had secured positions along the road facing the river. The fields widened considerably between the road, the buildings alongside and the river as it was viewed from right to left. Our riflemen maintained billets in cellars and out buildings with nothing between themselves and the enemy other than the Moder River and those six lonely cottages on the Rue des Pêcheurs.

To the left front was an expanse open fields stretching out several hundred yards, intermittently revealing field stone fences, concertina wire and an occasional shell hole, the evidence of earlier as well as more recent conflicts.

To the right flank, the intrepid Spearing and his crew held the ground from the bank of the Moder to the forward cottages at "Fish Street."

Shortly beyond that on the other side of the river were a sloping meadow, a tree lined ridge and a thicket of firs that went straight back into Oberhoffen.

It was in this wooded area less than 200 yards out that the Germans moved about so freely. Just beyond that area was Oberhoffen, teasingly spread out in front of us.

Our guys watched disconsolately as the enemy foot soldiers moved about while their motorized equipment rattled through ice and snow seemingly oblivious to our presence. They were a bit too far out for our snipers and small arms fire and not stationary enough for our mortars. Only our well placed time-fire and phosphorous seemed to keep them down for any period of time.

On the other hand, their observers had taken forward positions from the night before, were well-secured and hidden deep in V-trenches, and played constant hell with our more static positions. They called in the heavy stuff at our slightest movement. Again and again their eighty-eights slammed through plaster and timber. Again and again thatched roofs gave way. And "Haguenau Hattie" was always there to make her ominous presence felt.

Again the eerie squeaking came from Oberhoffen as a monstrous rail mounted gun rumbled up into position, fired, recoiled and squeaked back, its target somewhere off in the distance.

The rifle platoons' positions were not unlike those of the mortar section. They had claimed deep slit trenches that had been left by prior troops—both ours and theirs. Sgt. Paine with his platoon guide, Sgt. Wirt Glover, had secured positions at the west entrance of town on both sides of the road as it formed a "Y."

His squad leaders Cliff Miller and Gil Schaible billeted their troops in scattered cottages on both sides of the road leading off to the left and facing the Moder River. The enemy lines at Camp Oberhoffen were not quite visible from their line of sight.

Cows, goats and chickens were everywhere; the large animals overrunning Paine's positions had to be moved a couple of hundred yards south to where water troughs were available. The remnants of the other two platoons, less Spearing's squad, were dug in between the cottages and out-buildings which lined the bordering street. The G company line of defense formed a huge arc of over eight hundred yards in its entirety.

Starting perhaps twenty yards to the left of the CP, Sgt. George Snow and his devastated First Platoon consisting only of his platoon guide John Oddo, squad leader Don Vining, and a handful of others who took up their positions.

Two machine gun squads were dug in, one at the extreme left flank and the other perhaps eighty yards to the east and closer to Oberhoffen.

Their section CP was located in a house on the road just east of Sgt. Paine's positions and the gunners shuttled back and forth between the CP and their gun placements as their individual tours on a gun would dictate.

Sgt. Tom O'Neill with his gun crew, including Bill Kenny and Walt Pape, held down the left flank position, which was only reachable without exposure by crawling through a drainage pipe running under the road.

The pipe was barely wide enough to squirm through and brought claustrophobia from "your ass to your throat" for those who had to squeeze their way through the length of it, especially while under enemy artillery fire.

Sgt. O'Neill got caught up in that maneuver on one occasion. His arms were straight out in front of him and his canteen and other gear became temporarily lodged along the narrow sides of the drain. He "never went in that damn drain again."

The second gun placement was manned by Sgt. Jake Shenefield's crew, including Glenn Martin, and Wayne Scott. They were less exposed at the road but had to cross over considerable open ground to reach the gun itself. Their two guns covered the entire left flank and center in a crisscross traverse. It was at the second of these gun positions that Scotty died.

Lt. Shepherd's company command post was located near the inside right flank. Our main line of defense was now stabilized. The road, which made the "Y" to the left as we entered town and the lower ground between it and the river, was ours to control. Our front, center, and anything beyond was a "no man's land" and we planned to keep it that way.

We knew of their armor, halftracks, Tigers and armor plated command cars. Our intermittent machine gun fire, M1s, "borrowed" artillery and mortars kept them all pretty well occupied.

The small stuff was used cautiously as any untoward show of aggressiveness usually brought in all of Herr Schickelgtuber's available artillery and mortars. It wasn't any lack of will on our part, it was simply that we had become a helluva lot smarter.

There was one persistent Jerry, however, who managed to harass our lines more consistently than the rest.

At least we universally referred to "him" as only one even though "he" could have been many, each acting individually.

Any movement around the Company CP or Snow's area seemed to do two things. First, that "lone" soldat, well dug in at the edge of the woods, would spray an area with machine gun fire. We would respond with small arms and mortars, and "he" would already have pulled back. Invariably we would then be on the receiving end of at least one more volley of eighty-eight fire.

At night we would identify his muzzle fire and Lt. Shepherd would call in successive rounds of phosphorous and time fire directly on top of him, but "he" continued to come back, repeating the same tactic over and over from the same position and with our same response. If he was one "lone" kraut soldat he was one particularly mean, sonuva bitchin', diabolical bastard.

The village was slowly but surely being razed to the ground. Wood, timber and plaster piled awkwardly against solitary frames. Only a few farm animals were left to roam the village streets and those were deeply traumatized if not critically torn up.

THE REAR ECHELON

PIGS NO LONGER squealed and cattle no longer bellowed. The surviving chickens and rabbits were nearly all in control of Bob King, George Atkins, or our dairyman Clint Murphy.

The rifle platoon positions were not unlike those of the weapons platoon some twenty yards to the south side of the road. Riflemen took whatever comfort they could from the rooms within the cottages that remained standing just as long as the big guns and mortars stayed quiet. They did, however, hit the sanctuary of the beet cellars just the same as we of the "rear" did whenever the situation called.

The "rear echelon" syndrome was born from the deep pride that swells within the breast of every dog soldier belonging to a rifle squad. It's a simple, yet well accepted fact, that to the rifleman only his fire fights, glimpses at death and close calls counted. To him, it was he alone—or perhaps his platoon—who really knew where the war was or what it was about.

Everyone and everything else was "rear echelon" and "behind the lines." It was, therefore, easy to understand the slight feelings of contempt that were naturally predisposed between the rifle troops and the mortar section of which I was a member. This was true even though we were usually less than a few yards or so to their rear. Often when we couldn't avoid it we were also "the front."

The only other "dog faces" not seeming aware of this military truism were our counterparts in weapons: the machine gunners. They were, of course, a strange lot, and were all understood and expected to be a bit crazy. However, showing no partiality, they held equal contempt for the front and rear.

Our company CP was located in the cellar of one of those "frontline" cottages with its single entry opening out to the side and was some twenty feet adjacent to a slit trench manned by two rifle sergeants: First Platoon Sergeant George Snow (who was now by way of command also First Platoon Leader), and another Camp Gruber original, Sgt. Don Vining.

ANOTHER MAN
ANOTHER WAR

THE ENTIRE COMPANY area drew an extremely inordinate amount of enemy shell fire the evening of January 23rd, the day Scotty was killed.

For probably these two reasons and others of his own, Sgt. Lloyd Teale took a bare mortar tube, an apron of sixty milometer flares and struck out in search of a logical place to fire. Alone and intent on his mission, Teale wound his way past the company CP and toward Spearing's outpost.

Reaching "Fish Street," the Rue des Pêcheurs, he located himself in back of one of the last cottages. Mortar tube in hand with the ball to the ground, he aimed high out to the middle of the enemy lines.

He slid the mortars into the tube one after the other

and they leaped forward. Moments later, the flares exploded brilliantly over the open field in front of us. The night became day as though in complete awe at its own profound brilliance. Startled, the enemy began milling about in the wooded area just beyond, moving their lines, and pulling back vehicles. The rattle and creaking of their armored vehicles fell across the open meadow.

Grasping at the opportunity, Lt. Shepherd responded by calling in all the "borrowed" artillery he could muster and shortly thereafter the skies were again illuminated—this time, however, with our phosphorous and time fire, not theirs.

A great hole had been torn in the rear wall of the CP that morning before, and now became an open window to display the magnificence of their combined handiwork: first Teale's flares and then, under the lieutenant's orchestration, the time fire and phosphorous. Sgt. Graham watched in awe as one vehicle took a direct hit and its occupants flew into the air like so much baggage.

LIEUTENANT
LEONARD SHEPHERD

LATE THE FOLLOWING morning, at approximately 1100 hours, Lt. Shepherd (now the last of our original six company officers), our top kick First Sergeant Paul Graham, Sgt. "Dee Dee" Martin and radioman Milt Rogin, were alone in the CP.

Our telephone lines between the CP and the forward outposts had at one time been in place only to have been torn loose by a meandering cow. Therefore, the lieutenant, worried about his troops, determined that he and Martin would make physical contact with the outposts, leaving only Graham and Rogin to hold down the CP.

Graham had offered to accompany them but Rogin, ill at the time, was unable to man the radio. Because of this, First Sergeant Graham was to stay behind while the lieutenant and Martin struck out by themselves.

The lieutenant turned, took the few short steps up to the doorway, paused and stepped out into the late morning cold.

A single, silent mortar round slapped into the ground in front of him and between the slit trench occupied by Snow and Vining. A huge chunk of shrapnel tore through the air and ripped across the left side of his face and eyes.

Sgt. Martin immediately called out for a medic. Rifle Sergeant Vining started out of his hole to the lieutenant's aid when a second shell smacked into the mound in front of him. A part of the fin assembly tore into his jacket and threw him back into the foxhole he had shared with Sgt. Snow. Dazed, hurt, and knowing that he must have been wounded, he gingerly searched for torn flesh. His arm was badly bruised and his shoulder was slightly dislocated, but neither he nor Sgt. Snow found any blood.

The medic arrived and Sgt. Martin, concerned about the seriousness of the officer's wounds, left him with Graham and the medic and headed for the mortar placements to look for help. It was obvious that immediate transportation back to an aid station was needed.

SO MUCH FOR VOLUNTEERS

WHEN SGT. MARTIN entered the mortar section CP it was evident that something more than just another enemy shelling had gone down. There was anxiety mixed with excitement in the sergeant's voice as he told of us of lieutenant's needs and I remember something being said about a "volunteer."

I remember more succinctly, however, those deep penetrating eyes of Martin's as they burned a path directly into mine. I knew I was his "volunteer."

The battalion aid station was perhaps a kilometer south of us and to our rear. The road back skirted the edge of town and was in full sight of the German artillery and mortar observers over its entire length, and was well zeroed in on by their guns. North from this road one could look directly into the southwest gate of Oberhoffen.

Neither the sergeant nor I realized this complication until we hit this same road, on foot, perhaps halfway back to the aid station.

All hell broke loose and the eighty-eights poured in on the two of us volley after volley. The first three rounds were close enough to lift us off the ground as they tore their familiar patterns of grey, brown and blackened dirt into the snow cover about us.

Fortunately, they were completely surprised not only by our being there, but also by our strange and dedicated flight down a road which they so obviously held in their sights. Otherwise, the sergeant and I would have more than likely become just a bit more fodder for the French countryside.

First we could hear the rumble of their muzzle blasts from deep in Oberhoffen as the shells left their guns. We followed by going asses up and bellies down awaiting the devastating few moments it took for them to find their way into our hip pockets. The shells tore home covering us with bits of rock, dirt and blackened snow.

We would get up and run for a few paces before picking up the sound of more Oberhoffen guns and again we "hit the dirt." I tried again and again to pull the ground up over me.

We left the road and ran along its perimeter, but the shelling didn't let up. Wherever we went they followed us, every shell seemingly directly on top of the other and each as a direct hit.

The thought of returning for the lieutenant on this same route flashed through my mind and I dismissed it as something even my sergeant wouldn't think of let alone try.

Our first refuge was a group of buildings where our road intersected with another coming in from the west and away from the krauts and their visual pursuit.

As we closed the distance between ourselves and the Germans, an open Jeep appeared before us. It was made to order, unattended and parked in front of the first building on the right as we approached.

We hopped in, cranked it up and with the sergeant at the wheel, attempted to spin around and head back. The vehicle tied up in snow tracks and we were unable to head in the right direction. Undaunted, Sgt. Martin accelerated and headed straight back toward the gates of Oberhoffen, ass-end first!

Totally surprised at the sight of an oncoming vehicle bearing down on them "ass backwards," we had returned probably three quarters of a kilometer before they managed to throw one or two more volleys at us. Each of these went sailing over our heads, blasting far beyond and out of harm's way.

When we reached this point the road went directly left and west into town where the lieutenant waited. Here Sgt. Martin finally managed to turn the truck around and we headed properly back toward the CP.

The medic, Snow and Vining were still with the lieutenant when we slid to a halt. The lieutenant was propped up against a utility pole and freshly bandaged.

With the medic's assistance we managed to get the lieutenant loaded on the rear jump seat with me holding him upright. Within moments we were headed back up the road for the third time, once on foot and now a second time by vehicle. I was wrong—Sgt. Martin was definitely crazy.

This time they were really ready for us. As soon as we hit the bend and headed back toward the rear, they opened up again. The shells fell all about us, again in ominous volleys of three. Twice blasts came in so close that it lifted the Jeep and its quarter ton clean off the road! More than once I nearly lost the lieutenant as we jostled about down our trail of destiny, dirt and debris flying everywhere.

Our arrival at the battalion aid station turned us in and away from the krauts. Now, with their direct observation ended their artillery pursuit also stopped, and we managed to get the lieutenant into the hands of a medical clerk.

The sergeant cursed the orderly's need for detail. Only after being assured of the lieutenant's wellbeing, he ordered me back on board our borrowed vehicle. Now for the fourth time we set about to test Jerry's skill and our luck.

This time it wasn't just Cowboys and Indians—it could have been Barney Oldfield and a not too willing assistant driver taking on the Baron Von Hotstrasse.

We could have taken a route on foot a hundred yards or so inside of town and infiltrated through whatever buildings we found along the way.

However, that wasn't what old "Barney" Martin had in mind and off we went. This time, however, front end first.

Once again they were more than ready. I thought every gun in Oberhoffen was on us.

No more anticipating volleys of three, but a constant, never ending, consummate and relentless barrage of eighty-eights with a probable heavy mix of whatever mortars they could find.

Shrapnel tore at metal and tires. The concussion tossed us about like a cork on a stream.

I could barely hear my sergeant over the tumultuous din as he yelled out to prepare to jump as once again we headed directly into the gates of Oberhoffen.

We approached the turn into the center and, not slowing the least, "Barney" bellowed "jump" – and we did, ass over teacup.

I remembered a flash of concern for my dirt clogged carbine as I rolled over into the ditch and scrambled toward the safety of our mortar section CP some hundred and fifty yards away.

I entered the mortar CP awaiting the sound of bugles blaring. Didn't they know they had a real "Cowboy" in their midst? Sgt. Teale continued to bitch about Nickeson's sugar theft; Nickeson continued to make applesauce; Ray Schumacher watched; my best buddy Gene "Willie" Willson yawned and Phil Schaeffer slept. I guess nobody cared.

THE BREAKTHROUGH

WHEN SGT. MARTIN and I separated immediately after ditching the truck, I headed for our mortar CP in search of adored veneration and he plodded off for whatever sergeants do.

At 0100 the following morning, E Company, located just west of Kaltenhouse and defending part of the eastern perimeter of Haguenau, took a tremendous artillery and mortar barrage. Two hours later the enemy infantry began an attack with units of the once crack 21st SS.

Nearly 100 of these feared enemy troops were taken and the attack was broken.

Meanwhile, K and I Companies met the Tenth SS Frundsberg Panzer Division at still another point across Moder. There, just northwest of Kaltenhouse, the Rainbow MLR was even more sparsely stretched out.

American tank destroyer in action – Kaltenhouse

It was also there that I Company troops Walt Keeler, Elwyn Cole, Dee Eberhart, Pete Compton, Mike Kondroski, Jack Parry, Ted Simonson, John Nicoli, Herb Grossman, Karl Wagner, and "Pop" Lawson, along with others of Jim Birdsill's squad met the full brunt of this attack.

From their foxholes and zigzag short trenches "inherited" from past diggers they represented themselves, 3rd Battalion, 242nd Infantry and the Rainbow in true "Hero" style.

This sparsely defended line with its huge gaps of open

space was soon to be breached at the early onslaught. The platoon CP was hit with a sustained enemy offensive, but was defended successfully by Jim Freetly and Joe Dorsey.

Compton drove off a party of Germans who had sprayed a shallow ditched area with automatic weapons fire and percussion grenades. His only weapon was his formidable Ml rifle.

A dense fog rolled in during the heat of the fray and all was obscured. The cold damp air penetrated the troops from both sides. As a result, the small arms fire subsided. Only the imaginary enemy was targeted by small arms fire as the dense fog continued to hide the combatants one from the other. The heavy stuff continued; regardless, their targets were preset and locations of hostility on both sides were known.

As the fog lifted and the skies gave way to early morning light, the last flight of 242 Third Battalion troops took place. This time, however, it was only to secure better positions in the foxholes and slit trenches which lay between themselves and the slowing German troops.

Intense artillery and mortar fire continued from both sides and, during an appropriate lull, Sgt. Jim Freetly sent a wounded Lt. Poggi back with a cannon company truck.

Both K and I Companies had cleared themselves from the now blackened open fields, which had been covered with a fresh blanket of white from a snow fall just the day before. Now it was the enemy targets which were visibly wedged in. They were caught precariously between I and K Companies and had taken refuge in and about a factory and surrounding grounds just at the eastern outskirts of Haguenau.

At 1600 that afternoon, L Company with tank support attacked these positions. The enemy was tenaciously cut down while sustaining heavy losses of both dead and wounded. Many German prisoners were taken before they reached stabilized positions with a retreat back to the north bank of the Moder.

Dee Eberhart chronicled of I Company's involvement in that pre-dawn attack in his *Haguenau Reflections*: "No one was captured, most were not wounded, mistakes were noted and rectified; in the future hand grenades were kept handy and BARS were prevented from icing, a new defense line was formed, a successful counter attack was launched, a number of enemy were killed, wounded, and captured and all positions were recaptured late in the same day of the attack."

The Men of Love Company as portrayed in Sherman Ruesch's hard hitting book of that same name, were probably the most severely fraught by the enemy breakthrough.

During that same encounter on January 25th one

officer, Lieutenant "Moose" Yelton and eight enlisted men were killed.

The lieutenant died while attempting to gather his charges into stronger defensive positions. Ruesch's recall of fallen comrades that one day included Weapons Platoon's Szucs and Kruszynski, while the Third Platoon's Harrison and Stephenson went down with their lieutenant. The "First's" fatalities included Barry, Dickens, Labhart and Renard.

Love Company wounded on the 25th alone were; Boltz, Iwen, Leff, McGrath, Holcomb, Wheeler, Samit, Spernick, Syslo and Smith; eleven in all with visible wounds.

This one rifle company in one very memorable day at the front suffered twenty casualties, not including the ill and battle fatigued. This was an extremely heavy toll on an already hard hit company of the Rainbow's finest.

THE FINAL TWO DAYS

USING ALL OF their military logic, the Germans chose that prior evening and early the following morning as a moment in history for their last major infantry thrust, and it was there at the Kaltenhouse-Haguenau line.

It was now January 26, 1945, and the 7th and next to last full day of the Regiment's defense of the Moder River. Coincidently, that day also saw the end of the German "Operation Feuchtinger," which had its start in Hatten some two weeks and three days prior.

Confronting Lt. Shepherd's artillery and Teale's illuminating mortar flares had probably dissuaded the enemy; they determined not to make a direct assault across the Moder from Oberhoffen into Kaltenhouse itself

Instead they worked their way east some fifteen hundred yards or so and laid down a portable bridge. With their crossing at that point they reorganized and gathered to their intended unit strength.

Just across the meadow and along the Haguenau-Kaltenhouse road were the left flank of G Company and all that remained of F Company, now under the new command of Lt. Robert "Bob" Daly, recently assigned from G Company.

The thrust of the German attack came only after a considerable number of their troops had made their way across the Moder and had gathered strength there at its south bank.

After a misleading and well planned enemy artillery barrage was thrown directly east of that point and into Kaltenhouse proper, Jerry made the move toward F Company and flanking G Company 2nd Battalion lines.

They started across the lower meadows in a direct assault toward the Kaltenhouse-Haguenau Road leaving their armored and artillery in support.

Their attempt at deception failed. Even though totally outnumbered, Rainbow laid down a small arms counter that devastated the German ranks now left completely open in the meadows below.

In reference to that night twenty-one year old Clifford Miller of G Company wrote, "One night I was on OP they attacked us. They threw everything at us but the kitchen sink. We (the regiment) broke up the attack and took about 400 prisoners."

Miller's account, although short, very succinctly spelled out in but a few short words the success of our Kaltenhouse and Haguenau defenses and the initial bending of the German will to win.

The intended deception by the German bombardment of the G Company defensive positions deep into Kaltenhouse had its impact on G Company. Although it was merely a cover for a more immediate incursion of the American lines just to the north and east, it took its toll in Kaltenhouse.

One specific example was an incident involving Sgt. Spearing and Ed Gall. Spearing was with Ed Gall for first watch from their forward OP on the Rue des Pêcheurs. Gall was observing from the north window of their "open air living room," and Spearing from an east window across the same room.

They could hear the low rattle of an Oberhoffen tank moving right to left off in the distance. It paused momentarily to spit out its venom on some faraway target to the east. This brought about an observation from the sergeant that they would "probably get some sleep tonight."

The words had hardly left his mouth when there was "a red flash and blast" from just outside his window position.

Something smashed into his forearm, shoulder and left side. He was thrown violently to the floor, face up, his mouth and eyes were inundated with debris. He had been struck with fragments from one lone mortar shell fired singly, probably "for effect." It most certainly had been effective.

The sick nauseous feeling of shock crept through his body. Numbness enveloped his left arm. He glanced about quickly for his buddy, searching through the gloom and the dust filled room.

Boot soles pointing straight up disclosed Gall, not over a foot away, covered with rubble, and momentarily knocked senseless from the concussion.

Long moments passed before Gall, numbed with shock but untouched by shrapnel, gathered himself up and stumbled his way to the rear of the house. Here the rest of the detail had tried to find sleep on the kitchen floor.

Meanwhile the severely wounded Spearing dragged himself through the piles of plaster and timber to an open trap door and dropped himself into the shallow cellar below.

While the enemy barrage continued for several minutes, which seemed forever, the young sergeant gathered the courage necessary to examine his left hand and arm, which was now totally numb from the elbow down. With self-examination his hand appeared to be at least "there" and bleeding very little.

Shortly thereafter, Gall and the rest of the wounded sergeant's crew had joined him in the protective confines of the cellar and its pile of potatoes. Candlelight observation and deft examination disclosed that the bones of the forearm had been "snapped clean."

Claude Hawkins applied a splint to the injured arm. Johnny Frasell found the Sergeant's wristwatch nearby, apparently ripped from the sergeant's arm by a mortar tail assembly, which had slammed its way into his side.

The spent tail assembly was found nearby. Spearing declined it as an offered memento.

Intermittent enemy artillery and mortar fire continued for the next two hours and finally subsided.

Hawkins suggested that King and he make a run for the aid station with the wounded sergeant; without argument the three of them made their way out the back window.

They headed back up the hill and toward Kaltenhouse proper and Weapons' position. They managed but fifty feet or so when the enemy caught them with "ball" ammunition at ground level and tracers overhead.

Dissuaded by rounds whipping about their feet and

the mortars that followed, they quickly made their way back to the house, and once again to the comfort of the potato cellar.

The following morning the three of them successfully made their way back to the company aid station. First Sergeant Graham made it over from the Company CP where he and medic sergeant, Dave Weiner, bade Spearing farewell with encouraging quips about his "Million Dollar" wound.

It was poor payment for the past eight days from the Koenigsbruck schoolhouse, over more than twenty kilometers of forced marching across frozen roads, blown bridges and an arm nearly torn from his body.

His war was over, however. There followed stints with an evac hospital at Saarburg and surgery. More surgery came at the Second General Hospital, Nancy, and also Paris, and on to England's Oxford General for rehab and finally home on the Queen Mary and back with his loved ones.

Troops from the 314th Regiment of the familiar 79th returned to Kaltenhouse that last day, the 28th, and relieved all of the Second Battalion, including our G Company.

A much welcomed Lieutenant James R. "Bob" Collins, returned from an eight day hospital stint at the 304th Medical Battalion and assumed temporary company command.

We gathered together what little gear we still owned and on the morning of January 28, 1945 we loaded onto six-by trucks and headed for Marienthal and then Gélacourt, France, for our first two weeks off the line, for rest and reorganization.

In *Mission Accomplished*, S/Sgt John L. Reith and T/S William A. Vaughn wrote: "But Kaltenhouse had proved the turning point in our history. We had met the best the enemy had to offer, and we had defeated him. Never again were we to retreat with shattered morale and depleted ranks." In retrospect, and to quote from correspondence with a now mellowed "don't care for shit or shinola" Irish machine gunner, Tom O'Neill, we were a "ballsy bunch of kids." We were "well trained and disciplined," and we "did one hell of a job in fighting off more seasoned enemy troops who were better armed and supported than we." At Kaltenhouse we did it courageously and effectively, and seemingly never thought about the odds.

Epiloque:
Dachau/Allach
Concentration Camps

The following is a transcript of an interview given by Norman A. Thompson to the Surviving Generations of the Holocaust on July 14, 1995, at a reunion in Seattle, Washington in commemoration of the 50 year anniversary of the liberation of the Dachau and Allach Concentration Camps.

I was a mortar man in a rifle company, G Company of the 242nd Infantry Regiment, 2nd Battalion of Rainbow Division. Initially an ammo bearer in a five-man squad: squad leader, gunner, assistant gunner and two ammo bearers. Carried pretty heavy-duty ammunition in "apron" with six in front and six in back, 60 mm mortars, pretty good size shells, quite a bit of weight. I was a mortar-gunner, 30 yards behind the machine gunners.

Unit shipped over as a division from Camp Kilmer. Our initial combat was securing area around Strasbourg. There was a breakthrough and we were sent up to block that hole, as I understand it. You have to understand, I was a Pfc.—threatened to be broken down to a buck private a couple of occasions—we'll talk about that off-camera *[Chuckles]*. We plugged the holes and did what we could to stop that movement, referred to by our enemy as Nordwind *[Note: AKA Operation Nordwind]*, one of the last great offenses that Hitler had kind of personally become involved in, as I understand the history. We went in at company strength of 187; some three days later we were down to 47, many, many wounded, prisoners of war.

I lost three comrades in three days; they were close to me: Pat Patterson, driver Mark Markowitz, and Scotty. I'd like to be able to address their families, and I have not. I'd like to talk to them and express what I knew about them, especially Scotty, was a very personal relationship. *[Pauses; struggles to continue.]*

We reached a finger of woods in Gambsheim, one of our major conflict areas. My platoon became more of a rifle unit than mortars because we couldn't use our mortars.

Got up there with our carbines and M1s and fought along-side the riflemen and were moved up to an area known as the Ice Pond, where we lost so many troops. We held our position but finally had to pull out. I have great recall of at least twelve of us piling onto one Jeep, one of the only mobile facilities of getting out of there. We were attacked by tanks, had no support, no great deal of artillery, so we went into an area of woods, and those woods were just leveled above us. Tree bursts were just cutting, shearing trees. We were within two or three hours of getting back to what was referred to as the Landgraben Canal, and there we dug in and held our position for three days with a lot of shelling and a lot of misery, sending out a few squads into a combat arena to find out if the enemy was still around. We were relieved by the 79th Division and went immediately into another conflict at Hatten.

Hatten—it was even worse than Gambsheim for me personally—my only personal conflict, eyeball to eyeball you might say, with the enemy. We secured the first few houses at Hatten, and in an alleyway—we'd attacked from a place called Wiederschofen—night fell and up the alleyway came the German troops, not knowing we were there; they weren't even at arms, with their shouldered weapons. They had these white capes on. I immediately hollered out, *"Halt! Hande hoch",* which was something we'd been taught to do, sounded logical: Stop! Hands up. They just went in every direction. I had a carbine and emptied all my magazine at them as they spread and three were right in front of me in some shrub, and I emptied my first clip in that area. By this time my sergeant, Phil Schaefer, who had been sleeping, was wide awake. He stood by the window and I went outside and emptied another carbine in that general area. Unfortunately, hard for me to remember, there were some bodies out there. That was my personal involvement at that time, in Hatten.

From Hatten we pulled out *into* Niederbetschdorf and Rittershoffen, one combat after the other. Finally got 14th armored division in and they came in and whipped butt, if you'll excuse the expression. We pulled back into a little village [unclear] in Alsace, and brought troops back in and rebuilt our units, so I went back into combat as a gunner on the mortar squad. My buddy Willie Willson, we were still in the same squad together and on the first night out, on March 15 [1945] in what we referred to as the Push; we were attacking and the Germans were on the run. Our unit was going up a hill and the Germans were on the far side with tanks with eighty-eight mounts and they were firing down howitzers and a tree burst hit right above me, so I took shrapnel in my back and my butt and my leg.

One of my buddies along with Ray Schumacher, who

I believe was my squad leader at the time, helped me get down the hill. I wasn't hurt badly but was losing a lot of blood. I or one of them accidentally put a hand into the open wound and shock hit. I was taken to a gravel pit at the base of the hill, a lot of troops just lying there. One fellow who wasn't moving who I had cuddled up to get some warmth. I was in and out of it. Saw troop movement and thought, Thank God, I'll be picked up, but realized it was the enemy. I passed out again and don't remember anything until I woke up, this time looking at some boots and they were of German origin.

One fellow had a bad case of bronchitis; they made him take his jacket off and put rifles in the sleeves and put me in this hammock and they carried me off the field. I only had one more moment of consciousness and I seem to recall clearly one of the rifles had a white flag in it and they were waving it back and forth. I might have been with them for a couple of days at most. Next thing I knew I'm in an American field hospital near Ynette, France. From there I was transported to another field hospital. My war really literally ended for me without danger in Nancy, France. I was there for a month, then went to a replacement depot. That's where my involvement with Allach and Dachau began.

I'm searching for people who know more about Allach

than I do. It's right outside Dachau. It was either a camp in itself or was a satellite camp or it was a [unclear] Allach gate and someday somebody's going to be able to fill in those places. A lieutenant came into this replacement depot specifically looking for Rainbow Division veterans. I went forward and he said, "We're going to do something and it may have some historical value."

He didn't talk about concentration camps. We didn't know the words "Holocaust" or any of those terms. We knew displaced persons and prisoners of war, but that was about our knowledge of the camps. We knew those camps existed. They implied there wouldn't be any danger, that we were going in as a combat unit but the war was literally over and we wouldn't have any problems. Our arrival, I believe, was by trucks, or else we walked from the replacement depot. Had to be a very short distance. My first recall in Allach was the sign—and they're still there in the small villages throughout [unclear]—and they have the town name on them. I remember very clearly seeing "Allach" and noting it was double L.

Two hundred yards out and I started seeing the fence and people on the fence. Younger boys reasonably in good health; they were standing. I was on the right flank pretty much by myself. I heard some shots being fired to my left, maybe half a dozen. As we approached I could see these people behind four-inch mesh fence, they were calling out: "American! Cigarette?" I heard the word Polski. The lieutenant hand waved me over to an outbuilding, 20x40 shed that might have been an infirmary of sorts. As I was moving toward there I could see the tracks and the forty-and-eights and obviously stacked bodies outside. I have recall maybe by having seen a photograph of the doors being open on the side and I could see the bodies inside, but I have a difficult time in the real world of remembering having gotten that close to it. The sights were horrible enough.

I was to secure that building. I opened the door and there was nobody in, but as I went to the right there was a window and I looked down through the window and saw a man lying on a pallet in what could be referred to as a loincloth, couldn't have weighed 60 pounds, his head was shaved, his eyes were just orbs, inset in skin taut across cheekbones, elbows and knees were probably three times normal size, connecting to thighs no bigger than my wrists. He looked up and smiled. *[Thompson's voice cracks; he trembles and tears appear.]*

He couldn't speak. I expect that he lived. I stayed with him minutes; had to report to the lieutenant so somebody could get to the man.

It was just a matter of hours from when we arrived and

left. They were starting to bring up portable kitchen and showers, hospital unit. That was our duty and we were no longer there after that; other troops came in. Saw evidence of combat prior to our getting there; may have been suicide, or at the hands of people there. I did see two guards at one of the towers, 150 yards from gate. Bill Lowenberg, President's Commission on the Holocaust chair, was the only person I ever met who was in Allach. I met him recently in San Francisco where we were receiving the Yorn HaShoah medal for liberation. He said numbers he heard were 33,000 at Allach.

What message would you like to leave for future generations?

We as a people don't want to forget that that happened. It's the only way it won't happen again. Problem is it's kind of happening now. Bosnia, African nations. Where man's consideration of man seems so insignificant and so weakened. Right now I'm involved in and want to address groups in the middle school years. My message is one more of the fact of what happened and let them recognize in themselves what they might do. They are so interested; they need to understand and have tolerance of one another; we're not all the same—different ethnicities, different beliefs. Why should we have such destruction in the name of a religion or any other cause? They are more informed than I was as a kid.

In my 23 months in service I became an adult. There was a lot of patriotism then, but I wonder about that patriotism; is it because it was a word we learned to express or was it built on tolerance and love for other people? I don't think so. I don't think we really knew.

Allach Liberation – April 30, 1945

KALTENHOUSE REMEMBERED

Norm after the war